LIVING PROCESSES

Food Webs

Carol Ballard

rosen publishing's
**rosen
central**

New York

Published in 2010 by The Rosen Publishing Group Inc.
29 East 21st Street, New York, NY 10010

Editors: Sarah Eason and Leon Gray
Editor for Wayland: Julia Adams
Designer: Paul Myerscough
Illustrator: Geoff Ward
Picture researcher: Maria Joannou
Consultant: Michael Scott OBE

First Edition

Library of Congress Cataloging-in-Publication Data

Ballard, Carol.
  Food webs / Carol Ballard.
     p. cm. -- (Living processes)
  Includes index.
  ISBN 978-1-61532-340-1 (library binding)
  ISBN 978-1-61532-351-7 (paperback)
  ISBN 978-1-61532-352-4 (6-pack)
  1. Food chains (Ecology)--Juvenile literature. I. Title.
  QH541.14.B356 2010
  577'.16--dc22

                                 2009028379

Photo Credits:
Corbis: Reuters 39; FLPA: Jurgen & Christine Sohns 36; Fotolia: Anne Kitzman 12, Nicholas Larent 40, Red 30,
45; Getty Images: David Boily/AFP 35; Istockphoto: FotoIE 23t, Greg Gardner 38, Frank Leung 14, Stephen
Strathdee 37t; Photolibrary: Phototake Science 41t; Shutterstock: Galyna Andrushko 6, Ami Beyer 17, Jay Bo
16t, Rustam Burganov 11, Dennis Donohue 26b, Sonya Etchison 34, FloridaStock 41b, Andrey Gatash 37b,
Gilmanshin 10, Ben Heys 15, Javarman 4, 23b, Gail Johnson 29, J.Y. 5, 20, Mashe 3, 19t, Andreas Nilsson 21,
Antonio Jorge Nunes 13, Pakhnyushcha 32, Leigh Prather 8, Susan Quinland-Stringer 16b, Dr. Morley Read 9,
25, Rico 24, RTimages 42, Elisei Shafer 7, Audrey Snider-Bell 22, James Steidl 19b, Luis César Tejo 18.
Cover: Istockphoto/FotoIE.

Manufactured in China
CPSIA Compliance Information: Batch #WAW0102YA: For Further Information contact Rosen Publishing, New York, New York at 1-800-237-9932

SAFETY NOTE: The activities in this book are intended for children.
However, we recommend adult supervision at all times since neither the
Publisher nor the author can be held responsible for any injury.

Contents

CHAPTER 1

Food for life

Every living organism—from spiders and trees to seaweeds and tigers—needs food. Food provides vital chemicals that allow an organism to grow and stay healthy. It also provides energy for basic life processes and activities such as movement. Different living things get their food from different sources.

Food for plants

Green plants can make their own food using the energy from sunlight. This process is called photosynthesis. Green plants also need water, minerals, and trace elements, which they get from the soil they grow in. The roots of the plant grow down into the soil and absorb water, along with any minerals and trace elements that are dissolved in it.

Some plants and plantlike organisms get some or all of their food from other sources. Parasites live on other living things and obtain some or all of their nutrients from them. For instance, the mistletoe is a parasitic plant that grows on apple and other soft-barked trees.

Food for animals

Animals cannot make their own food, so they get the nutrients they need by eating plants or other animals. Their food must provide them with everything they need to grow and stay healthy, as well as meeting all their energy needs. Most animals live off the food sources available in their habitats. Some animals are also parasites and live in, or on, other animals, stealing nutrients from their hosts. For instance, tapeworms live in the intestines of animals such as pigs. The tapeworms absorb nutrients from the food that passes through the host's digestive system.

Animals and plants live in a wide range of habitats, from dry deserts to salty seas.

ANIMAL NUTRIENTS

Have you ever wondered exactly what minerals, trace elements, and vitamins are?

Minerals and trace elements occur naturally in rocks and soil. Both play an important part in keeping an animal healthy. Minerals are substances that animals need in large quantities, such as calcium to build healthy bones. Trace elements are essential for life, but animals do not need as much of them. Selenium and zinc are trace elements.

Vitamins are complex organic chemicals. They are called organic chemicals because they contain an element called carbon. Plants and some animals can make their own vitamins. Humans can make some, but not all, of the vitamins they need.

All living organisms, from seaweeds to sharks, need food to stay healthy.

Finding out what animals eat

There is a lot of different evidence that shows us what types of food a particular type of animal eats. Some evidence comes from the place where the animal lives. Other evidence comes from the animal itself, for example, from prints, teeth, tracks, marks, and waste.

Habitat and location

Animals live in places where the type of food they need is plentiful. Looking at the habitat provides clues about the type of food an animal eats. For example, a squirrel naturally lives in the forest, where it has access to a good supply of nuts.

Animal evidence

Animals leave evidence that we can use to discover what type of food they have eaten. These include:

Prints and tracks: prints and tracks around a carcass or other remains can reveal which animals visited the site. The size of the tracks will indicate the size of the animal—in general, the bigger the animal, the bigger its feet. The shape of the tracks is also important. For instance, badgers have five digits, foxes have four, and deer have two.

Teeth marks: each type of animal has a distinctive arrangement of teeth. Teeth marks of different shapes and sizes can be used to identify an animal.

Squirrels store excess acorns in the summer and the fall to provide them with food in the winter, when it is scarce.

Animal waste: different animals leave different types of waste, and this can help to identify them. Herbivores feed on similar types of plant food, but their droppings are often distinctive. Some droppings can also reveal what type of food has been eaten, for example, if the waste contains undigested seeds.

The location of the waste is also important. Badgers dig pits and deposit their droppings in them, but foxes simply leave their waste on the ground.

Rodent bones are often found in barn owl pellets. These clues tell us more about the animals the owl eats.

INVESTIGATE:
Animal evidence

Animals leave telltale clues when they are searching for food or eating. A badger makes a small hollow in the ground where it has been searching for bulbs. A fox leaves bird feathers with chewed ends in piles, and a sparrowhawk leaves a circle of undamaged feathers. Owls cough up pellets that contain bones and fur. These can be used to identify what the owl has eaten. Slugs and snails leave slime trails and chewed-up leaves.

Take a look in your yard, local park, or school playground. Can you see any evidence about animal feeding habits? Record your evidence in a table like the one below. If you have a camera, you could record each piece of evidence that you find in a photograph.

evidence	where I found it	what it tells me about animal feeding
chewed leaf	backyard	animal eats plants

CHAPTER 2

Plant producers

Green plants need three things to perform the process of photosynthesis: water, carbon dioxide, and sunlight.

Without water, photosynthesis will slow down and eventually stop. A plant's roots absorb water from the soil. The water is carried through special tubes, called xylem, up the stem to the leaves.

Carbon dioxide is a gas that occurs naturally in the air we breathe. The gas enters plant leaves through tiny holes called stomata. Increasing the amount of carbon dioxide available to the plant will increase the rate of photosynthesis.

The cells of green plants contain tiny structures, called chloroplasts. The chloroplasts contain the chemical chlorophyll, which gives plants their green color. Chlorophyll traps energy from sunlight. Photosynthesis speeds up when there is more sunlight, but too much can damage chlorophyll. Some plants that grow in very hot, bright places have a red pigment, which acts as a sunscreen and prevents any damage to the chlorophyll.

Plant producers

Photosynthesis uses the energy from sunlight to combine carbon dioxide and water into a sugar called glucose.

Leaves have large surface areas to trap as much sunlight as possible for photosynthesis.

The reaction releases oxygen as a by-product. The process can be shown as a simple equation:

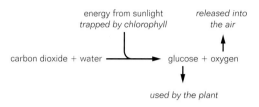

energy from sunlight trapped by chlorophyll — released into the air

carbon dioxide + water ⟶ glucose + oxygen

used by the plant

It can also be shown as a chemical equation with symbols:

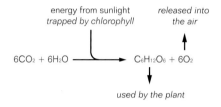

energy from sunlight trapped by chlorophyll — released into the air

$$6CO_2 + 6H_2O \longrightarrow C_6H_{12}O_6 + 6O_2$$

used by the plant

Food factories

Most of photosynthesis takes place in the leaves—the plant's food factories. Palisade cells on the upper surface of the leaves contain more chloroplasts than other types of plant cells. They are therefore able to photosynthesize more.

Maximizing the light

The leaves of most plants are flat, providing a large surface area to trap the sunlight. In large plants, such as trees, the leaves can overlap and shade each other. Trees usually arrange their branches to reduce the overlap effect. Most plants also move their leaves depending on the direction of the sunlight.

Effect of temperature

In most plants, the rate of photosynthesis is fastest within the normal temperature range of the habitat the plant lives in. At very high temperatures, photosynthesis may even stop. Generally, most plants cannot photosynthesize below about 39°F (4°C), so they stop growing in the winter.

DECOMPOSERS

Fungi share many features of plants, but they do not have any chlorophyll and cannot photosynthesize. They get their nutrients in a different way—by breaking down the bodies of dead plants and animals. This is called decomposition, and fungi are known as decomposers.

This fungus cannot make its own food like a plant. It gets its food from the tree on which it is growing.

The onions people eat are bulbs that grow at the base of the onion plant.

Bulbs

Bulbs and corms (see below) may look similar, but they are very different. Bulbs are made up from layers of tightly packed leaves. They serve as a food store from which new plants can develop. Onions and garlic are both examples of bulbs.

Stems

Some plants store food in structures called corms and tubers, which are swollen underground stems. Corms grow year after year, producing new plants with more corms. Crocuses are an example. Tubers grow into a single plant, which then produces many tubers. Once the tuber has produced a new plant, it rots. Potatoes are tubers.

Fruits and seeds

Many plants reproduce from seeds. When conditions are suitable, the embryo in the seed starts to develop. The developing embryo needs a supply of nutrients. One or two structures inside the seed, called cotyledons, support the new plant until it can produce its own food.

Storing food

Plants usually make more food than they can use and store the excess for the future. Most store food in the form of a chemical called starch. Many plants use starch as a food store for germinating seeds, so they can grow and develop before the seedlings start to produce their own food by photosynthesis. Different plants have different ways of storing the surplus starch.

Roots

Many plants store food under the ground in their roots. The roots can survive in the soil during the winter, and then give rise to new plants in the spring. Vegetables such as carrots and parsnips are swollen roots.

INVESTIGATE:
Plant oils

Cooking oils, cosmetics, inks, lubricants, paints, and pesticides—plant oils are used to make many different products. Find out more about plant oils and their uses. Conduct a survey of all the plant oils that are used in your house each day. To do this, you will need to check the labels of every product used for washing, cleaning, and cooking. Record your results in a chart like the one below. How many different plant oils do you use? Are some used for more than one purpose?

product	contains oil from	used for

Some seeds are enclosed or embedded in soft, dry, or hard fruits. Lemons are soft fruits, beans are dry fruits, and walnuts.are hard fruits. Seeds can survive for long periods if the conditions are not quite right for germination, for example, in a drought or severe winter conditions. Some can survive for thousands of years. Scientists managed to germinate the seeds of an arctic lupin that were 10,000 years old, as well as 2,000-year-old magnolia seeds.

The seeds of the sunflower plant develop within a large flower head called an inflorescence.

Animal feeding

Animals that eat only plants are called herbivores. They do not all eat the same parts of the plant. Some eat roots, leaves, shoots, and stems, and others eat nectar, sap, fruits, nuts, and seeds. Some eat a wide variety of plants, but others eat just one. They all have special features that make them well suited to their diet.

Leaf, shoot, and stem eaters

Some herbivores eat the leaves, shoots, and stems of plants. Grazing herbivores, such as cattle, sheep, and goats, tear up or snip off the short stems and leaves of ground-level plants. They use their strong, flat back teeth to grind down the plant material. Some have a digestive system designed to extract the maximum amount of nutrients from their food. Giant pandas feed almost entirely on bamboo shoots, stems, and leaves. They have front paws with a special thumblike structure that is designed to hold bamboo shoots. Giraffes have long, flexible necks to allow them to reach the leaves on high branches.

Nectar eaters

Many flowers produce sweet liquid, called nectar, which is an excellent source of energy. Hummingbirds have adapted to feed on this nectar.

A hummingbird beats its wings up to 200 times a second to hover by a flower and feed on its nectar.

Many have long, thin beaks that can probe deeply into the flower and suck up the nectar. They can also hover in the air close to the flower. Many insects, including bees, butterflies, and moths, also feed on nectar.

Sap eaters

Many insects, such as aphids and leafhoppers, feed on sap, which is a sticky liquid inside plant tissues. The mouthparts of these insects are designed to pierce the plant tissue and suck the sap from inside.

Monkeys have opposable digits in the form of a thumb and fingers, which means they can peel a banana with ease to feed on the fruit inside.

Fruit, nut, and seed eaters

Many different animals eat fruits, nuts, and seeds. Tiny animals, such as caterpillars and slugs, crawl inside the fruit. Monkeys carefully peel fruits such as bananas. Blackbirds and many other birds peck at fleshy fruits such as apples, or they may carry off berries and other small fruits. Many rodents, such as squirrels, have sharp front teeth to break into hard nuts and seeds.

DARWIN'S FINCHES

The English naturalist, Chárles Darwin (1809–1882), visited the Galápagos Islands in 1835. He studied some of the islands' birds, called finches. The finches were all very similar in many ways, but birds living on different islands had different beak shapes. Darwin concluded that they had all evolved from a seed-eating finch.

Each island provided the bird with a different type of food, for example, seeds on one island and berries on another. The finches with the beak shape best suited to the island's food source thrived, but finches with other beak shapes gradually died out. Darwin's studies of the finches played an important part in his theory of evolution by natural selection.

Eating meat

Carnivores are animals that eat other animals, from fish and insects to birds and their eggs. Carnivores can be divided into smaller groups, depending on the types of animals they eat. For instance, piscivores eat only fish, insectivores eat only insects, and ovivores eat only eggs. Omnivores eat a varied diet that includes both plants and animals.

Fussy feeders

Some carnivores can eat only meat and no other type of food. Cats are an example. The digestive system of a cat cannot break down plant material, for instance. When cats do eat plants, it usually makes them sick.

Lions are top predators of the African savannah, feeding on zebra and other prey.

Daggerlike teeth line the jaws of this dog's skull. The dog uses them to hold prey in a powerful grip and slice up their flesh.

When carnivores such as lions and hyenas eat, they use their powerful jaws and sharp, pointed teeth to tear and slice up animal flesh. Strong molar teeth also help them crush hard bones.

Our choice

Most people are omnivores and eat a varied diet. They might eat a ham sandwich, apple, and yogurt for lunch. The ham is meat, the yogurt is made from cow's milk, and the apple and the grain used to make bread come from plants. Vegetarians do not eat meat but may consume animal products such as milk. Vegans do not eat any animal products.

SNAKES

Can you imagine trying to swallow a melon whole, complete with the skin and seeds? You wouldn't be able to open your mouth wide enough to fit it in, and you certainly couldn't swallow it without chewing. Yet snakes do this every time they eat. Snakes are carnivores and swallow their food whole, head first.

Snakes can swallow prey much bigger than their own heads. They do this by dislocating (separating) their upper and lower jaw, so they can then open their mouths very wide. The skin around the jaws is stretchy, too. The snake's teeth curve backward, so as a snake moves its jaws around its prey, the teeth fix into the prey and gradually work their way over the body.

Corn snakes usually feed on small mammals such as rodents. The snake will feed every few days to get the nutrients it needs.

Many animals are omnivores like people. They eat whatever food is available in their habitat. Bears, pigs, monkeys, raccoons, and woodpeckers are all omnivores.

Filter feeders

Some animals are filter feeders. They live in the sea or freshwater habitats, take water into their bodies, and filter out tiny organisms in the water. The filter feeder digests these tiny creatures and then expels the waste water. Oysters, jellyfish, flamingos, herrings, and basking sharks are examples of filter feeders.

Scavengers

Some animals do not hunt and kill their own food. Scavengers eat the foods left by other animals. When a lioness kills a gazelle, she may eat some of the meat and leave the rest for later. If a scavenger such a hyena passes by, it will steal some of the lion's kill. The hyena has a free meal, without having made much of an effort.

Scavengers often eat the remains of dead animals. Crows, coyotes, skunks, and opossums all eat road kill (animals that are killed by traffic). Some seagulls and crabs scavenge on seashores.

Vultures are probably the best known scavengers. They plunge their bald heads deep inside rotting carcasses without getting any mess stuck on their feathers. Vultures can feed on decaying meat that would be completely inedible to most other animals.

WEIRD THINGS!

Scientists have found some organisms that do not make their own food by photosynthesis, nor get nutrients from other living things. One is a bacterium called *Desulforidis audaxviator,* which was discovered 1.7 miles (2.8 km) below Earth's surface in a South African gold mine. The bacterium uses radioactive uranium from the rocks around it. Uranium releases hydrogen and sulfate compounds. The bacterium combines sulfate compounds with carbon and nitrogen from the rocks and chemicals from the water. It then uses these combinations of chemicals to make proteins.

Black vultures use their sharp beaks to tear flesh from the remains of a dead animal.

Detritivores

Some animals, called detritivores, feed on the decomposing remains of dead plants and animals. They clean up the bodies and their waste products. Many detritivores live in soil, others live in fresh water, and still others in salt water. Millipedes, earthworms, freshwater shrimp, and wood lice are examples of detritivores.

The body of an earthworm is a simple tube. It has no jaws or teeth, and uses its muscles to suck soil into its body. The earthworm grinds up the soil and absorbs any nutrients in it. The undigested soil then passes out of the earthworm's body as a worm cast on the surface of the ground. As earthworms feed, they loosen the soil, making it easier for air and water to enter. This improves soil fertility.

As they feed, earthworms break up the soil, which lets in air and water. This makes it easier for plants to grow.

Millipedes use their many legs to burrow through the soil and feed on the decaying remains of animals and plants.

CHAPTER 4

Eat or be eaten!

Some plants have adaptations, such as the thorny stems of roses and the spiky leaves of holly, to stop animals from eating them. Other plants produce poisons to immobilize any animal that eats them.

Stinging nettles inject poison into the skin of animals that touch them. Chrysanthemums contain pyrethrum—a natural insecticide that kills aphids. Bracken leaves contain a powerful poison called cyanide! Some plants produce chemicals that are not poisonous but taste very bitter. For example, chili pods have a very hot flavor that deters most animals, apart from humans. Other plants have waxes or resins that make them hard to eat.

Colors and patterns

Animals and plants use colors and patterns to blend in with their surroundings and hide from animals that might eat them. This is called camouflage. Living stone plants, which grow in South Africa, are hard to see in a pile of pebbles, so grazing animals often overlook them. Other plants grow to resemble their more dangerous relatives. Dead nettles are harmless, for instance, but they look very similar to stinging nettles, and animals usually avoid eating them.

Some animals feed on the nectar produced by flowering plants. For example, bees gather nectar from flowers and use it to make honey. They store the honey as a food source for the winter. Some flowers have bright-colored petals to attract a variety of nectar eaters.

The fronds of a bracken plant are poisonous, which protects them from being eaten by herbivores.

Others attract only one type of pollinator. For example, the flowers of the bee orchid are shaped like a female bee to attract the male.

Many common flowers that look plain to human eyes may look very different to insects. They may see attractive markings that lead to the center of the flower, like airport runway lights. People can only see these markings under ultraviolet light. Nocturnal insects emerge at night and will not respond to visual cues. Instead, they may be attracted to flowers that produce distinctive scents.

Waxwings breed in northern temperate forests, feasting on the abundance of berries in the area.

INVESTIGATE:
Animal helpers

Some plants rely on animals to eat and digest their fruits. Their seeds pass through the animal's digestive system unharmed and end up in the animal droppings. Most animals wander around in search of food, so they often disperse the seeds a long way from the parent plant. Fruits need to attract animals to eat them for this system to work.

Find a hedge or other collection of plants and look for berries, fruits, and seeds. Draw a table similar to the one below to record the characteristics of your finds, such as color, structure, and texture (for example, soft or hard). Can you figure out what types of animals are attracted to the different plant parts?

name of fruit, berry, or seed	color	texture	structure	other features	how would it attract animals?
olive	green	hard	fleshy	conspicuous	tasty flesh

Predator or prey?

Animals that hunt other animals are called predators. The hunted animals are called prey. Predators have adaptations to help them find and catch prey. Prey animals have adaptations to avoid being eaten. So there is a battle for survival between predators and prey.

Looking for prey

Predators need to be able to locate, catch, and eat other animals. They rely on their senses when hunting prey. Most predators have eyes at the front of their heads, which gives them a good forward view. Some can spot food from vast distances. For instance, a sparrowhawk has 20/2 vision. This means the sparrowhawk can see at 20 yards (18 meters) what a human with normal eyesight can see at 2 yards (1.8 meters).

Other predators rely on good hearing to listen to the sounds made by prey. For example, owls have excellent hearing. Stiff feathers around the owl's face make two funnels that direct the sound of prey animals into their ears.

Some predators use other senses to detect their prey. Sharks have such an acute sense of smell that they can detect one drop of blood diluted in one million drops of water! Sharks also pick up the electrical impulses produced by fish as they swim. Snakes called pit vipers have heat sensors on their heads, which can detect the heat given off by animals.

This diamondback rattlesnake feeds on small mammals, such as rabbits and rice rats. The snake uses heat sensors on the head to home in on its prey and strikes with its venomous fangs.

Avoiding detection

Some predators use other tactics to avoid detection. Camouflage helps to avoid being seen. The mottled pattern on the body of the copperhead snake looks like dead leaves. This helps to break up the body shape of the snake as its lies in wait for prey. The mottled fur of the lynx enables it to hide against tree bark, ready to leap out at unsuspecting prey.

It is important to avoid being heard, too. Many predators move very quietly.

The rain forest frog shoots out its long tongue to catch prey, such as crickets.

Owls glide through the air so that their prey is not alerted by the sound of wing beats. Similarly, lions have soft paws that make little noise on the ground as they stalk their prey.

ECHOLOCATION

Bats hunt in the darkness, so eyes are not much help when locating their insect food. Most bats use a navigation system called echolocation to overcome this problem. The bat emits a sound through its mouth or nose. The sound travels through the air and bounces off of any objects in its path. The bat then listens carefully for the echo.

information from the echo	what it tells the bat
time taken for the echo to return	how far away the object is
difference in timing between the right and left ear picking up the echo	the direction from which the echo came
which part of the ear picked up the echo	the object's vertical position
strength of the echo	how big the object is
pitch of the echo	from which direction the object is moving

The bat's brain can pinpoint the exact location of a flying insect by piecing all of this information together.

Prey adaptations

Prey animals rely on a variety of methods to avoid being caught by predators. Camouflage is a good way of hiding from predators. Leaf insects and walking sticks are hard to see in the dense green vegetation they live in. Similarly, the mottled skin of flatfish such as the flounder blends in with the sandy sea floor. With its masses of soft, flexible fronds, the leafy sea dragon looks like a piece of floating seaweed. The giant swallowtail caterpillar has a brown-and-white pattern that makes it look like bird droppings—and not many predators want to eat them! Some animals can even change color to blend into the background. For example, a lizard, the green anole, changes color from green to brown as soon as it moves from green leaves to brown branches.

Super senses

The earlier a prey animal can detect a predator, the greater its chances of survival. Many prey animals have highly developed senses of sight, smell, or hearing. They need to keep a lookout because a predator could approach from any direction. So their eyes are usually at the sides of their heads, giving them a good all-round view. Large ears and a keen sense of smell also help them to detect approaching predators.

Defense

Since predators also have keen senses to help them to find their prey, prey animals rely on other defense methods to stay alive. Some use chemicals to ward off predators. For example, a skunk sprays foul-smelling chemicals at predators, and an octopus releases a cloud of black ink when it feels threatened. Poison dart frogs secrete chemicals from their skin that are highly poisonous. Likewise, the long, sharp quills of a porcupine will deter most predators.

Cuttlefish ink was once an important natural dye called sepia.

INVESTIGATE:
Warning colors

Many animals use warning colors to put off predators. As its name suggests, the red-backed poison dart frog is highly poisonous. The frog's red back acts as a warning to predators that it is dangerous. Other animals copy these warning signals but are harmless. This is called mimicry.

Look at some books and use the Internet to find out how animals use colors and markings to avoid being eaten. Record the information in a chart like the one below. In the last column, try to explain how the colors and markings of each animal might deter a predator.

animal	markings and colors	how they deter predators

Do some combinations of markings and colors seem to be more common than others?

Poison dart frogs get their name because tribes in the Amazon rain forest use the frog's toxic secretion to poison the tips of their blow darts.

Escape

A predator can only eat what it can catch, so many prey animals move quickly to avoid capture! An octopus escapes in a burst of speed by squirting a high-speed water jet out of its body. A cheetah is the fastest predator on the land. It hunts gazelle on the African savannah. The gazelle cannot match the cheetah for speed. Instead, it makes sharp, abrupt turns to outrun the cheetah.

Hunting tools

Once a predator has found its prey, it needs to attack before the prey can escape. Predators therefore need to move very quickly. One of the fastest predators is the peregrine falcon. It can dive through the sky at 180 miles (290 kilometers) per hour. The cheetah can reach speeds of 62 miles (100 km) per hour. Some predators have body shapes that suit hunting particular prey. For example, the long, slender weasel can move easily through the tunnels of small mammals such as mice and voles.

An eagle uses its razor-sharp talons and beak to catch and tear apart its prey.

The puma races at high speed to catch its prey, then jumps onto its back to pin it down and kill it.

The predator has to attack and subdue its prey once it has caught the animal. Size and strength can work to the predator's advantage. Razor-sharp teeth and claws, talons, and hooked beaks are also good hunting tools. For instance, golden eagles kill deer calves and other small mammals by stabbing their sharp talons into the ribs and back. Storks use their sharp beaks to stab and kill fish. Pumas leap onto the back of their prey, killing them with a single bite to the neck.

Trapping prey

Some animals lay traps to catch their prey. Most frogs have long, sticky tongues that shoot out rapidly to grab hold of insects. Spiders build webs to capture prey. Others use the silk to build different traps. Funnel weaver spiders spin flat mats and wait in a funnel at the end of the web. When an insect lands on the mat, the funnel weaver spider moves in for the kill. Trapdoor spiders hide in a tunnel with a flap at the end. The flap opens when an insect walks over it, and the spider grabs the insect.

Some animals work together to trap their prey. Several lionesses will hunt in a pack. One lioness lies ready to ambush the prey, while the others chase it toward her.

BUILDING ORB WEBS

To construct an orb web, the orb web spider exudes a single silk thread that catches on a branch, twig, or other support. It then exudes another thread that loops down. A third thread hangs down from the center of the loop. This structure forms the main support of the web. The spider produces more threads that run from the center of the web to the outer threads. It then creates a sticky spiral between the supports. The spider moves around on the nonadhesive support threads, while the adhesive spiral catches the insects. When the spider sits in its web, it can sense the tiny vibrations of a trapped insect.

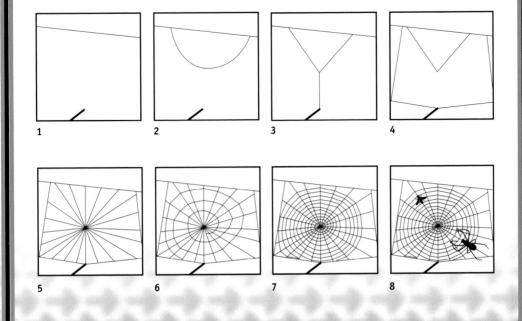

1   2   3   4
5   6   7   8

CHAPTER 5

Food chains and food webs

Food chains describe the feeding relationships between different living things. Most food chains start with plants. Plants produce their own food using the energy from sunlight. They are called producers. Animals eat plants and other animals. They are called consumers.

When you write down a food chain, you draw an arrow between each organism. The first arrow points from the producer to the first consumer. The second arrow points from the first consumer to the second consumer. Each arrow means "is eaten by." Look at this food chain:

grass ➜ rabbit ➜ fox

The grass is a producer. The rabbit, which eats the grass, is the first consumer. The fox, which eats the rabbit, is the second consumer.

Longer food chains

Most food chains have more links than this. For example, the food chain for a pond habitat might be:

pondweed ➜ tadpole ➜ water beetle ➜ small fish ➜ large fish ➜ otter

The pondweed is the producer, and the tadpole, a herbivore, is the first consumer. The water beetle, small fish, large fish, and the otter are the second, third, fourth, and fifth consumers. The otter is the last consumer in the food chain. It is called the top carnivore.

Other beginnings

The first living thing in a food chain is not always a green plant. Some food chains start with dead animals, which are eaten by scavengers:

dead shellfish ➜ crab ➜ seagull

Food chains can also start with dead plants, which are eaten by detritivores, such as worms:

dead leaves ➜ earthworm ➜ American robin ➜ hawk

In this food chain, the arrows mean "'is eaten by." You can see that the pondweed is eaten by the tadpole, which is eaten by the water beetle, and so on.

pondweed   tadpole   water beetle

INVESTIGATE:
Predator, prey, or both?

Almost all food chains in nature contain animals that are both predator and prey.

dead plant and animal material ➡ earthworm ➡ shrew ➡ barn owl

In the food chain above, the shrew is a predator because it eats earthworms. It is also prey for the barn owl. Look at some books in your local library and use the Internet to find some food chains that contain animals that are both predator and prey. Make a chart like the one below to show each animal, how it has adapted to avoid being eaten, and how it is adapted to hunt its own prey. Do some adaptations help in both circumstances?

The barn owl is at the top of its food chain. It has no natural predators.

animal	prey adaptations	how they help it avoid being eaten	predator adaptations	how they help it catch its prey
shrew	dull color	camouflage	sharp teeth	strong grip

Not so simple...

The feeding relationships between different organisms are usually much more complicated. Very few creatures rely exclusively on one type of food. Some are mainly herbivores but will occasionally eat animal material. Some are both carnivores and scavengers, hunting for food and eating the leftovers of other predators. Some omnivores will eat just about anything.

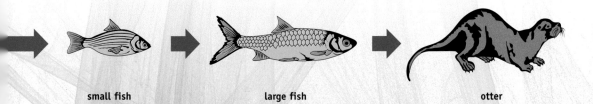

small fish   large fish   otter

Energy transfer in food chains

Animals and plants need energy to perform basic life processes. Plants trap energy from sunlight. This energy is transferred from the plant to each consumer in the food chain. However, some of this energy is lost at each trophic level (point in the chain).

Pyramid of numbers

Think about how many organisms there might be at each level in this food chain:

plankton ➔ small fish ➔ salmon ➔ brown bear

Each small fish will eat countless individual plankton. Each salmon will eat many small fish. A single brown bear will eat many salmon. You can illustrate this

information in a diagram called a pyramid of numbers. Each box shows the number of organisms at each trophic level. In this particular food chain, the diagram forms a pyramid shape.

However, the pyramid of numbers for some food chains can look very strange. Look at this chain:

rose bush ➔ greenfly ➔ ladybugs ➔ swallow

The first trophic level consists of a single organism—the rose bush—but many greenfly will feed on the rose bush. So the bottom level of the pyramid will be much smaller than the levels above. The pyramid of numbers shows the number of organisms but does not reflect the size of each organism.

The brown bear is at the top of its food chain pyramid. One bear may catch as many as 90 salmon in one day.

Pyramid of biomass

A pyramid of biomass is a diagram showing the total mass of the organisms at each trophic level. If you draw a pyramid of biomass for the rose bush food chain, the result would be a proper pyramid.

Although there is only one organism in the first trophic level, a rose bush, its mass is much bigger than the combined mass of the greenfly that feed upon it. In turn, the combined mass of the greenfly is greater than the combined mass of the ladybugs. And the combined mass of the ladybugs is greater than the mass of the blackbird.

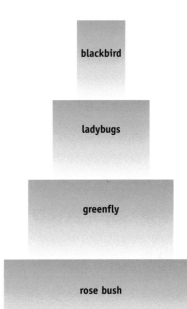

The rose bush food chain shown as a pyramid of biomass. The rose bush has the greatest mass and the blackbird has the smallest.

LOSING ENERGY

Energy is lost at each trophic level as you move through a food chain. There are three main reasons for this:

1. Consumers in one trophic level do not eat all of the food from the trophic level below. For instance, a herbivore might eat only the berries of a plant but not the leaves. Similarly, a carnivore might eat the flesh and skin of the prey but leave the bones.
2. Consumers expend energy by moving around and keeping healthy.
3. Some energy is lost as feces and urine.

Eventually, the energy loss means that there is not enough energy in the food chain to support another trophic level.

Linking chains

Food chains are a good way of representing feeding relationships, but they do not reflect the complexity of nature. In any one habitat, there may be several different food chains at work, and some animals will appear in more than one chain. Scientists have to look at all the food chains together to get a balanced view of all the feeding relationships within a habitat. This can be shown in a diagram called a food web.

Woodland habitat

Look at these food chains:

seeds ➡ mouse ➡ fox
seeds ➡ mouse ➡ owl
seeds ➡ finch ➡ sparrow hawk
green leaves ➡ rabbit ➡ sparrow hawk
green leaves ➡ rabbit ➡ fox

There are two types of plant material: seeds and green leaves. These are the producers. The mouse and finch eat the seeds. The rabbit eats the green leaves. So the mouse, finch, and rabbit are first consumers. The fox and owl eat the mouse, the sparrow hawk and fox eat the rabbit, and the sparrow hawk alone eats the finch. These are the second consumers, or top carnivores. Instead of showing five separate food chains, the information can be put together into a food web.

Longer and shorter chains

The five food chains in the woodland habitat all have three elements. When these food chains are arranged in a food web, the trophic levels are easy to identify. However, some food chains have more elements:

green leaves ➡ snail ➡ thrush ➡ sparrow hawk

A woodland habitat contains many different plants and animals, which are linked together by a food web.

In this food chain, green leaves are in the first trophic level, and the sparrowhawk is in the top trophic level. But there are two trophic levels in between—the snail and the thrush. Adding this food chain to describe the feeding relationships in the woodland habitat will complicate the middle levels of the food web. But all natural habitats include a range of different food chains. Complex food webs are therefore common.

This food web shows how the food chains at work in a woodland environment feed into the web.

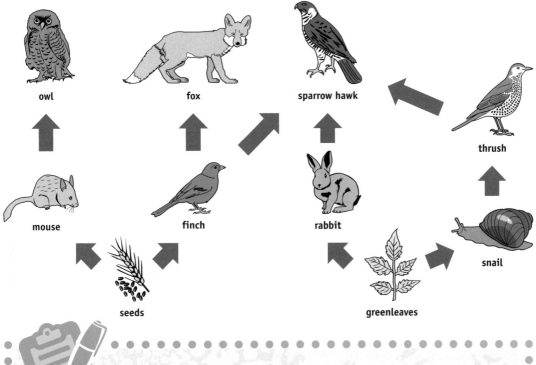

INVESTIGATE:
Looking at food webs

Food webs can be used to illustrate every natural habitat, from the dry deserts and salty oceans to snow-capped mountains and humid rain forests. Study the different organisms in your yard, local park, or your school grounds. Try to build a food chain. You might see greenfly clustered around a rosebud. A ladybug on the rose bush might be eating the greenfly.

Can you see any birds that might eat the ladybug? What else might the birds eat—slugs or worms? Can you see a predator that might hunt the birds—a cat, for example? Try to build up your food chain from the evidence you find. Explain how it works. If you have a camera, you could take pictures and put them together to illustrate your food chain.

CHAPTER 6

Changes to food chains and food webs

Feeding relationships are constantly changing. The populations of individual plants and animals in any given habitat change with time. Other factors such as the availability of food may lead to an increase or decrease in the population. Any change to one population of organisms will affect every other organism in the food web.

An increase in the heron population would affect every organism in its food chain.

Changing numbers

Look at this freshwater food chain:

plankton ➜ shellfish ➜ fish ➜ heron

Think about some of the things that could change in this food chain. The top carnivore is the heron. If the heron population increases, more fish will be eaten. The fish population will then decline. Fewer fish means that the shellfish population will increase. They then will eat more plankton.

If the fish population increases, they will eat more shellfish. The population of shellfish will decrease. Fewer shellfish means that the plankton population will increase. One change in a trophic level affects all the trophic levels in the food chain.

HUNTING

People often alter the balance of food chains and food webs by hunting wild animals. In the Arctic, polar bears are one of the top carnivores. The bears mainly hunt seals, but they also eat other animals, such as eider ducks. If humans hunt seals, the polar bears lose a vital food supply. They will eat any other food they can find, but there will not be enough for them all. Some bears will starve. Even though people were not hunting them directly, the polar bears will still die as a result of their actions.

Restoring the balance

Nature usually restores the normal balance in the food chain. Consider the first scenario, when the heron population increases. Eventually, the herons will run out of fish to eat. They will either move on to find food elsewhere, or they will starve. The heron population will return to the original level, and the populations of other animals in the food chain will be restored.

Seal hunting by humans reduces the polar bears' food supply.

Too much damage

Sometimes, the damage is too great. If the herons ate every single fish in the population, there would be a missing link in the food chain. The natural balance of the habitat would be permanently disrupted and the food chain destroyed forever.

Natural competition

Different animals often eat the same type of food. Unless there is plentiful supply, animals will have to compete for the food resources. In the African savannah, cheetahs, leopards, and lions, as well as some other animals, compete for herbivores such as antelopes and gazelles. Similarly, birds such as sparrows and finches might compete for plant seeds in your yard. If one animal is more successful at competing for food, other animals will suffer.

Animals and plants compete for scarce resources, too. For instance, woodland plants such as bluebells grow and flower early to make the most of the available sunlight before the expanding leaf canopy shades them out. Many animals defend a territory in which there may be a plentiful supply of food.

Seasonal changes

Many plants and animals respond to seasonal changes. Plants may follow an annual cycle of maximum growth during the spring and summer, flowering in the summer and fruiting during late summer and fall. Consequently, the range of plant foods available to animals changes with the seasons. Shoots, leaves, stems, and nectar are plentiful in the spring and summer, and berries, fruits, grains, and nuts follow in the fall. In the winter, few plants are available as a source of food. Herbivores have several ways of coping with this winter food shortage.

Many animals, such as dormice, store body fat before the winter. During the winter, they enter a period of inactivity, called hibernation. Hibernating animals do not feed. Since they are hidden, they are not available as food for predators, and so the population of predators may decrease in the winter.

Leopards compete with other carnivores for food such as antelopes and gazelles.

Hoarders, such as squirrels, collect and store food before the winter and then return to it when they need it. Unfortunately, other animals may also eat the stored food.

Some animals, especially birds, migrate to warmer lands, where there is plenty of food. This so-called outward migration takes animals out of the food web, so they neither eat nor are eaten. Inward migration also occurs, when animals move into the habitat. Inward migration introduces animals into the food web. They will compete with inhabitants for food, but others may also hunt them for food.

Canada geese migrate to warmer climate zones every winter, returning in the spring when the weather gets warmer.

INVESTIGATE:
Seasonal changes

Find out about a habitat near you. How does it change from season to season? How will these changes affect the animals that live there? How will the changes affect the feeding relationships between them? Record your information on a chart like this:

season	habitat changes	effects on other plants and animals	effects on feeding relationships
summer	pond dries up	move to new pond	food chain disrupted

Environmental factors

Environmental factors can have a serious impact on a habitat and the organisms living within it. This disturbs feeding relationships and unbalances food webs, affecting the populations of different species.

Direct human actions

Human activities have a direct effect on habitats and wildlife. Many farmers use herbicides, pesticides, and chemical fertilizers to increase their crop yield. Crop spraying often spreads to other areas. Agricultural runoff occurs when these chemicals leak into rivers and other water habitats. The herbicides used to kill plants that farmers regard as weeds disrupt the food web, because animals rely on these plants as a source of food. Similarly, pesticides kill insects that farmers regard as pests, but they disrupt the food web by killing a source of food for other animals.

Accidental pollution

Sometimes accidents destroy the natural environment. Oil spills, industrial accidents, and leaks of human or agricultural waste can devastate the populations of local plants and animals. Large industrial sites may release chemicals into the air that travel vast distances in the wind and eventually settle on the soil. So the feeding relationships in areas far from the source of the pollution can also be disrupted.

Crop spraying can affect all organisms in a food chain, from the plants at the bottom of the chain to the predators at the top.

The fish in this river in central China have died because the river has been polluted by chemical waste from a factory.

Pollution in action: pig waste

Waste from livestock such as pigs may be kept in huge, open-air lakes or lagoons. If a leak or overspill occurs, the contents could potentially pollute the environment. In 1995, a pig waste lagoon burst in North Carolina. Over 29 million gallons (110 million liters) of waste spilled into the New River, killing millions of fish and severely disrupting feeding relationships in the area.

INVESTIGATE:
Pollution

Pollution can affect many different habitats and the food chains and webs that exist within them. Go to your school playground or local park and look for evidence of pollution. It could be litter from an overflowing trash can. How will the litter affect the local animals and plants? Draw a chart like the one below to record your findings. Then link some of the animals and plants in food chains. How might the litter affect the food chains?

type of litter	plants or animals it might affect	how they might be affected	how this could affect the food chain
plastic bag	small mammals	suffocate	missing trophic level

Bioaccumulation

Bioaccumulation describes the buildup of chemicals within in food web. Chemicals that are released into the environment often end up in lakes, rivers, and other watery habitats. The plants that live in the water, or whose roots absorb water from the surrounding soil, soak up these harmful chemicals. The chemical concentration in the plants may be very low. But if a herbivore eats a lot of contaminated plants, a tiny amount of the chemical enters its body each time it feeds. Over time, the concentration in the herbivore's body builds up. The chemical then passes on to any predator that eats the herbivore. Again, each time the predator eats a contaminated herbivore, the concentration in the predator's body increases. Eventually, the animal at the top of the food chain can suffer from a toxic, and sometimes lethal, dose of the contaminant.

BIOACCUMULATION IN ACTION

Clear Lake is a large freshwater lake in California. Between 1949 and 1950, scientists poured large volumes of a pesticide called DDD (dichloro-diphenyl-dichloroethane) into the lake to eradicate the gnat population, which people regarded as pests. At first, it seemed to work. But then the bodies of a freshwater bird called the grebe started to wash up on the shores of the lake. Scientists who examined the dead grebes found that their bodies contained high levels of DDD. When the gnats returned the following year, DDD was again poured into the lake. An important food chain in the Clear Lake habitat is:

plankton ➜ minnows ➜ perch ➜ grebe

The plankton took up the DDD. Bioaccumulation of the pesticide up through the food chain led to the demise of the grebe.

The death of grebes on Clear Lake was a direct result of toxins passing through the food chain from producer to consumer.

Water fleas feed on algae in lakes and ponds. Any chemicals in the water build up in the algae and pass on to the water fleas when they feed.

tissues. Other contaminants include agricultural chemicals, such as DDT (dichloro-diphenyl-trichloroethane), and industrial chemicals such as PCBs (polychlorinated biphenyls) and dioxins. In many countries, governments have now banned these chemicals to protect the environment.

Bioaccumulation in action: bald eagles

Bald eagles are top carnivores. DDT accumulation in female bald eagles leads to production of eggs with very thin, fragile shells. The eggs crack during incubation, and so the young die. The population size declines with each generation. DDT was banned in the United States in 1972.

Chemical cocktail

Only chemicals that do not break down in nature can build up in living organisms. Metals, especially arsenic, cadmium, and mercury, have been found to accumulate in animal

The bald eagle population has started to recover now that DDT is banned in the United States.

Build a food web

There are many different habitats on Earth. Choose one that you find interesting. Perhaps you would like to find out about the different relationships between the animals and plants of the rain forest. Or maybe you are attracted to the frozen lands of Antarctica.

A rabbit is a consumer. It feeds on plants such as grasses.

1. Look up some books in your library or surf the Internet for information about the habitat you choose.

2. Make notes about which plants live in your chosen habitat. Record what kind of food each might provide, such as seeds, nectar, leaves, or fruits. Write each one on a piece of card and then cut it out.

> **FOREST**
> (Habitat)
>
> **Provides:**
> seeds, fruit, nuts, plants

3. Make notes about the animals that live in your habitat, including insects and other small creatures as well as larger animals. Carefully record the name of each animal and some details about the food it eats. Write each one on a piece of card and then cut it out.

> **RABBIT**
> (Herbivore)
>
> **Eats:**
> plants

4. Lay your plant cards in a straight line. Sort your animals into carnivores, herbivores, and omnivores. Line up the herbivore cards above the plant cards. Try to arrange them so that each card is next to the type of plant it eats.

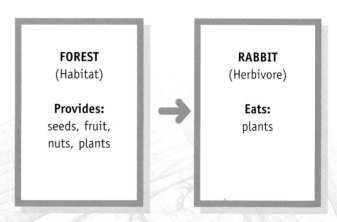

> **FOREST**
> (Habitat)
>
> **Provides:**
> seeds, fruit, nuts, plants

> **RABBIT**
> (Herbivore)
>
> **Eats:**
> plants

5. Find the carnivores and omnivores that eat the herbivores. Line up the cards above the herbivore cards. Try to arrange them so that each card is above, or close to, the type of herbivore it eats.

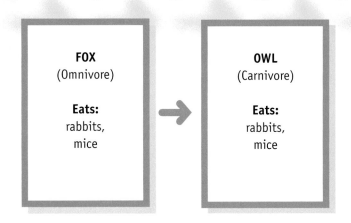

6. Arrange the remaining carnivores above the animals they eat.

7. Look at all your cards. Start with a producer and see how many food chains you can follow up through the layers of cards. Link each organism in the food chain with a piece of yarn or string.

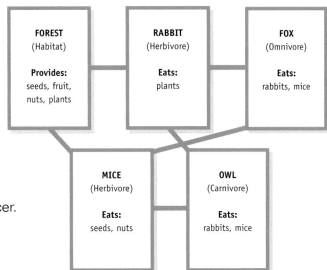

8. Do the same for each producer. You might need to rearrange some of the cards to make the chains easier to follow.

DYNAMIC WEB

Food webs are constantly changing. To investigate how a web may change, remove one card and all the links to and from it. What effect does this have on the rest of the food web? Will some animals starve? Will some have to compete for food?

You can make a permanent record of your food web in several ways:
1. stick the cards and links onto a large sheet of card
2. copy the names and links onto a large sheet of paper
3. copy the names and links on a computer

Glossary

adaptation Characteristic that helps an organism survive in its habitat.

bioaccumulation Buildup of chemicals through a food chain.

biomass The mass of an organism or group of organisms.

bulb Leafy food store from which a new plant can develop.

camouflage Hiding by blending in with the surroundings.

carnivores Animals that eat the flesh of other animals.

cell The basic building block of all living organisms.

chlorophyll Green pigment found in the cells of green plants.

chloroplast Organelle in green plant cells that contains chlorophyll. Chloroplasts are the site of photosynthesis.

consumer Any organism that eats another organism.

corm Modified underground stem that acts as a food store from which new plants can develop.

decomposer Organism that breaks down dead plant and animal material.

detritivore Animal that feeds on decomposing plant and animal material.

echolocation Finding an object by detecting the echoes of sound waves. Bats and dolphins use echolocation to find prey and move without bumping into things.

evolution Process by which every living thing slowly changes over time.

fungi Plantlike organisms that do not contain chlorophyll and so cannot make their own food. Mushrooms, molds, and yeasts are fungi.

germinate/germination When a seed starts to grow.

glucose A type of sugar.

habitat Place where an organism lives. There are many different habitats in the world, ranging from mountaintops to the ocean depths.

herbivore Animal that eats plants.

hibernation Dormant state during the winter or cold season.

migration Movement of animals in search of food or shelter, often as a response to seasonal changes.

nectar Sweet liquid produced by some flowers.

nutrients Substances that organisms need to live.

omnivore Animal that eats plants and animals.

organism Any living thing, such as an animal, plant, bacterium, or fungus.

palisade cell Plant cell that contains many chloroplasts.

parasite Organism that lives on or in another organism.

photosynthesis Process by which green plants trap energy from sunlight and use it to make food from carbon dioxide and water.

pollution Anything that, when added to something else, spoils or harms it.

predator Animal that hunts another animal for food.

prey Animal hunted for food.

producer Plant that makes its own food using the energy in sunlight.

sap Juice inside plant stems and leaves.

scavenger Animal that eats the food left by other animals.

trophic level Position in a food chain or food web.

Further information

BOOKS

Food Chains and Webs by Andrew Solway
(Rourke Publishing, 2007)

Food Webs: Interconnecting Food Chains
by Susan Heinrichs Gray (Compass Point Books, 2008)

WEB SITES

Due to the changing nature of Internet
links, Rosen Publishing has developed an
online list of Web Sites related to the
subject of this book. This site is regularly
updated. Please use this link to access this
list: http://www.rosenlinks.com/lpr/fweb

Index